T0381116

SOUL INFLUENCER

A Lightworkers Guide

KIM ILLINGWORTH

BALBOA.PRESS

A DIVISION OF HAY HOUSE

Balboa Press books may be ordered through booksellers or by contacting:

Balboa Press
A Division of Hay House
1663 Liberty Drive
Bloomington, IN 47403
www.balboapress.com
844-682-1282

Because of the dynamic nature of the Internet, any web addresses or links contained in this book may have changed since publication and may no longer be valid. The views expressed in this work are solely those of the author and do not necessarily reflect the views of the publisher, and the publisher hereby disclaims any responsibility for them.

The author of this book does not dispense medical advice or prescribe the use of any technique as a form of treatment for physical, emotional, or medical problems without the advice of a physician, either directly or indirectly. The intent of the author is only to offer information of a general nature to help you in your quest for emotional and spiritual well-being. In the event you use any of the information in this book for yourself, which is your constitutional right, the author and the publisher assume no responsibility for your actions.

Any people depicted in stock imagery provided by Getty Images are models, and such images are being used for illustrative purposes only.
Certain stock imagery © Getty Images.

Print information available on the last page.

ISBN: 979-8-7652-5305-2 (sc)
ISBN: 979-8-7652-5306-9 (hc)
ISBN: 979-8-7652-5304-5 (e)

Library of Congress Control Number: 2024911615

Balboa Press rev. date: 07/26/2024

To my incredible husband, Joe,
who has supported every silly idea I have ever had
and who has allowed me to grow into the lightworker I came
here to be:
I love you beyond love.

To my children Eliot, Abigail, and Joe,
who have taught me the most:
I made mistakes but I loved them with
my whole heart and still do.

And to my grandchildren Brooklyn, Nora, Indi Kai, Emma,
and Memphis:
you are my blessings in this life.

My family has been my reason for everything.
What a beautiful life this is, and I am so grateful.

Contents

Preface

I am a lightworker, a Reiki master teacher, and an angel intuitive. My passion is to help other people when they are struggling. I have survived depression, anxiety, and an addiction to alcohol. My desire to help people took me on a spiritual journey, and I am guessing that you have been on this journey as well. If you have a heart to help others, you are probably a lightworker. A lightworker is someone who is empathic and has a deep compassion for others. They love helping people. When I first started out in life, I had some adversity, which ended up giving me a lot of baggage and trauma. The pain from this caused me to develop an addiction to alcohol and numbing myself. The pain manifested in different ways, such as depression, anxiety, and eventually a pain disorder called fibromyalgia. When conventional medicine could not help me with my addiction or my fibromyalgia, I had to figure out how to heal myself.

Early on my journey, I read a book by Louise Hay called *You Can Heal Your Life*. It taught me that a lot of our physical illnesses are caused by emotional and mental pain. I began learning spiritual principles and committed myself to getting well. It was a long journey, but I slowly started to feel better, lighter. The more I helped myself, the better I felt. The addiction went away, and the fibromyalgia became manageable. As I found myself healing, I was compelled to tell others so that they could heal too. I realized as I healed my soul, I healed my body and mind.

I was introduced to energy healing because of my interest in alternative healing methods. I learned Reiki to heal myself and started helping others find healing. I was never sure I had the special magic other Reiki practitioners had, but I kept practicing. So trust me when I tell you that *you* have what it takes to be a healer and lightworker—you were born with it. You just need to agree to start healing yourself, and then help others on your way!

A lightworker is someone who has a heart to help and can lead people out of the darkness. They are able to do this because they themselves have struggled and are finding their way out. I'm fifty-five years old now, married with three children and five grandchildren. My life is so blessed. I have been sober for seven years, which have been the best years of my entire life. I understand energy now, and I realize that I can teach others how to manage their energy and their gifts. It was only about ten years ago when I first heard the term *lightworker*. A lightworker is an advanced soul who came here to help the evolution of Earth. Most lightworkers have a difficult life and at some point do the healing work on themselves.

In my early forties, I started learning energy healing and became an addictions counselor. I got certified in Reiki levels 1 and 2, Reiki master, and Reiki master teacher. I became a yoga teacher and got a mentor who helped me heal and release my trauma—I needed a new story, because trauma had become my story. All this healing raised my vibration and my desire to help other people find the peace I was finding. I stepped into my power, and I want you to step into yours too!

When I got sober, I started hearing angels. At first I thought it was my own thoughts or opinions. Over time I was able to figure out when it was my own thoughts and when it was the angels speaking. It took me three years to trust that the angels were giving messages to me and my clients. When I finally started telling my clients what the angels were saying, I saw the effect it had on them, and it was profound. I began calling in my client's angels as well as my angels before every Reiki session.

My angels helped me write this book by channeling their guidance to me. This book was initiated by them, so I can't take full credit for it. I entrust my life and everything I do to the angels every day, and I go where they guide me. I know I am always supported and never alone. My family has been incredibly supportive of my Reiki journey, and I am lucky they are so respectful of my work. They have to deal with clients coming in and out of the house, and they need to be quiet during those sessions. What an incredible thing to be supported by the people you love! They are the wind beneath my wings, and I am so grateful for them.

I hope this book blesses your heart and shows you that you, too, are a lightworker and a soul-influencer. I want you to remember how powerful you are in this world, and I hope you learn as well how loved you are. I am honored to be on the front lines of bringing the love back to this world with my fellow lightworkers. The earth is shifting back to love—it must in order for us to survive. Shine your light in this world for others to see. Shine in the darkness to give hope and guidance. You are here to do great things! Ask your angels and guides to show you how that looks and help you find your way.

Thank you for choosing to read this book. I honor your spirit and compassionate heart. With love and compassion, we can change this world. I will ask you to start seeing yourself with love and compassion first, so that by loving yourself you can overflow that love onto others.

Introduction

Working with angels and divine guides is an experience unlike any other. Each of us vibrates at a certain frequency based on the law of physics that tells us that we are made of molecules moving around at a certain frequency. When we feel good and are healthy we are in a higher vibration and when we don't feel good we are in a lower vibration. The vibration of angels and divine guides is very high. When I was drinking and in my low vibration, I could not hear my divine team. When I first heard them, I thought I was losing my mind because I was receiving thoughts in my head randomly without actively thinking. These thoughts came throughout the day but accelerated when I was helping someone. As I became able to tell the difference between my thoughts and the angels' words, I saw what an amazing gift it was. This is when my Reiki practice started to become transformative..

We all have a team of angels and guides.

The angels are here to help us learn, grow, and evolve. We each have a guardian angel and others on our team as well. Most of us have more than one angel, and we can also have ascended masters like Jesus or Buddha. We may have loved ones in spirit on our team too. We were not sent here alone to fend for ourselves in this difficult world. We have a team of divine beings who are our "staff" sent to help us on our mission here .Our angels came here to help us live out the mission we chose before we came. They remember that mission, even though we forget. Angels want us to ask for help all day, every day. They are here for us and focused on us 24–7.

As I started telling my clients what their angels were saying, it was as if I could see a light bulb come on in their eyes as they were remembering. The angels are expedient and get right to the root of our problems. Angels usually do not provide yes or no answers because they are out for our evolution and want us to learn. They give us suggestions through our intuition on where to go for our highest good. Angels have a way of wrapping their wings around us and helping us make the right decisions. They gently guide us to make the best decision, and they know that when we come to the conclusion ourselves, the change will be more permanent.

We can all receive messages from our angels and guides.

After I have given my clients their angel messages and we have an intention for our healing session, I give them a sound healing. After the sound healing, I do hands-on energy healing. I use Reiki and Integrated energy therapy (IET) to help bring my clients back to energetic balance. As a lightworker, I have chosen energy healing and angel intuition to help my clients find their way back to their soul. I am a soul influencer, and you can be one too.

You do not need to learn Reiki or go to school to do energy healing, but there is so much to know about energy healing that it is sometimes helpful to take classes like Reiki. You are already connected to God/Source and have the power of the Universe in you, but learning Reiki or other healing modalities is a good idea. It's like being in another country and knowing the language. If you are in another country and not able to speak the language, you can get by using hand gestures and a translation app, but it is much easier if you have an inner knowledge of the language. Reiki teaches you the language of energy and how to become a clear channel for that energy.

If you are an empath and have a compassionate heart, you are probably a lightworker. I was told a while ago by my angels that empaths and lightworkers would come to me to remember who they were and why they came here. Most of my clients are empaths and lightworkers and just haven't realized it yet. My job is to remind them of who they are and why they came, and then to help them heal. My angels told me I needed to reach more lightworkers, so I wrote this book. If you are reading this book right now, you are probably a lightworker.

In order to start healing others, you need to work on your own healing. I love my job, but it took forty years to figure out why I came here and what I was supposed to do. My hope is that you can find out sooner than I did and heal quicker too. I recommend that you commit to healing your trauma and pain, and as you do you can help others. There are many ways to do lightwork in the world, and you can start looking into all the different ways to see which resonate with you. Hands-on energy healing is my passion—energy healing is so powerful, and we can all do it. You were born with gifts. You just need to learn how to use them. I learned to help others heal, and it is such a joy to me. When you give energy healing, you actually receive it too. As energy healers, we are channeling universal life-force energy from Source. This energy channels through us to our client, so we receive healing energy as well. Isn't that incredible? I actually feel better when I give a lot of Reiki, and I notice that when I don't have many clients, I feel a bit low.

You have unique and special gifts, and you are an individual unlike any other. I hope after reading this book that you remember why you came here, that you remember the lightworker that you are. A lightworker's gift is the gift of love and compassion, and these are the highest-vibrating emotions we can have. Your lightwork in this world will look different from mine, and that is perfect. Each of us is a thread in the tapestry of life. When we go back to where we came from, we will be shown a "life review," which is like a movie of the life we lived here. If you are a lightworker, your review will show the times you helped people and loved people. We all came here to learn, and sometimes some of our biggest learning experiences are the most painful ones. We win when we can take those painful healing experiences and help others to see their way out into the light. We are guides and teachers.

Angels need to be asked in order to help because they give us free will. They will allow us to go off the path, but they love to help guide us back to the path we chose before we came. You are never too old or too young to be a lightworker, so start now! Don't deprive this world of your contributions for one more day. If you wait until you are healed to heal, you may never help others. Your light is needed, and it is so beautiful. Be a soul influencer for good. I use energy healing and guidance from angels in my work, and you will learn ways that you, too, can be a healing facilitator and lightworker. I will walk with you on this path of lightwork. I am linking my arm around yours for the journey.

YOU ARE A LIGHTWORKER

Trust me, if you are reading this book right now, you are a lightworker! A lightworker is someone who has compassion for others and wants to help. They have an incredible heart and are compelled to make others' lives easier. These advanced souls feel the need to take other people's pain away. Lightworkers are here to bring light to a darkened world by helping one person at a time. These compassionate souls tend to have careers in service to others; for example, teachers, nurses, doctors, social workers, or therapists. Lightworkers also take a spiritual path where they learn about things of a supernatural nature. "Supernatural" means things that are beyond human capability, things that are not "natural."

You may have already started on this path to enlightenment. You have a desire to learn why you are here and what the meaning of life is. You question this world, and you don't agree with the status quo. You always may have felt "different" or as if you were separate from others. You may have thought that you were here for a reason and to do something important. You wondered this because you are—you are here to help the world change for good.

Maybe you have preferred to get alternative healing modalities like acupuncture or use holistic medicine. You like natural remedies and feel you can heal yourself. Lightworkers always find their own way and then share that information with others. We use the name "lightworker" because, energetically, a lightworker downloads light from God/Source and spreads it here on earth. You are a lighthouse, and people tend to tell you their life story right away. You may have been reading the energy around you your whole life without realizing it. If you have a hard time in crowds or get overstimulated, you may be an empath and lightworker. You may always be concerned about others before yourself.

Lightworkers are usually empaths. An empath is someone who picks up on other people's emotions and energies. They are very sensitive to others and tend to put themselves in other people's shoes to understand what they are going through. This level of care for others is rare, and that is what makes empaths and lightworkers incredible catalysts for healing in the world. You are qualified to be a lightworker when you have this kind of compassion. Once you know you are a lightworker, you need to go out into the world and show the world your gifts. What are those gifts?

There are so many different ways to help people. Follow your passion to find the way that's best for you. If you love exercise, yoga, and taking care of your body, you may become a yoga teacher. If you love to help people when they are sick, you may become a nurse, doctor, acupuncturist, or naturopath. If you are a good listener and like to help people by giving constructive advice, you may become a life coach or a therapist. Your passion may be for animals, and you may become an animal intuitive or animal energy healer. If your passion is for plants or trees, you may become a master gardener or farmer. If you are compelled to keep our earth healthy, you may become a scientist who finds ways to protect the health of the planet. If you love to write, you may become a writer of books. If you love astrology, you may teach people about astrology charts and their signs. Maybe you want to learn about past lives or the akashic records. Lightworkers help the world by communicating in various media, as Glennon Doyle and Abby Wambach do with their podcast *We Can Do Hard Things*. They are lightworkers who reach millions of people with important messages.

I wanted to help people with hands-on healing. When I was in college, I took lessons from a nurse about healing touch, and years later I became a Reiki practitioner. My first reaction when someone needs help is to touch them. There are infinite ways to be a lightworker. When you research different ways to help and you find something that sparks your interest, learn it! In my practice I use Reiki and an angel healing modality called integrated energy therapy (IET). I use sound healing as well as messages from my clients' angels in my sessions. When I first learned Reiki, I just did Reiki and nothing else. My sessions evolved over time with the help of my divine team. It was a joy to learn different ways to help people, and I am still learning. All lightworkers have a team to support them here on Earth. We all planned our life before we came here, and lightworkers had a plan to help people heal.

It would be wonderful if you can make your lightwork into a career, but you may have a separate career and do lightwork on the side. Being a lightworker usually does not come with benefits like insurance or retirement funds, but you will get eternal rewards. My spiritual journey started with Reiki, and when I learned Reiki, I learned about energy. I was interested in crystals and learned about all the different crystals and their properties for healing. I became interested in life after death—where do we go when we die? I started studying people who had died and come back after a near-death experience (NDE). I am a huge fan of Anita Moorjani, who had end-stage cancer and was at the hospital, dying, when she left her body and had an NDE. When she came back, she healed completely from the cancer and has made it her life's mission to tell people what she learned. I encourage you to read her books! I have read and watched so many people share what they saw and learned on the other side, and their stories about going to heaven and coming back have given me so much peace about dying.

One book I studied is *Your Soul's Plan* by Robert Schwartz, in which he explains that we have a soul team in heaven and we plan our life with them before we come here. Some of his ideas were challenging—after all, that would mean I had planned all the awful things that have happened to me in this life. I learned that we choose to come here to learn and to live in a physical body. On the other side, or what you may call heaven, there is no pain or judgment. You won't even have a body; you will be energy. I wondered why we would choose to come to live on earth if it is so painful. I believe that our soul wants to be the best soul it can be. You can call it karma or Christ consciousness, but it is simply wanting to be the best soul we can be. Most likely we want to be the highest-vibrating soul. So you come here to learn lessons, and when you do, you become a more advanced soul.

But why would you choose to go through pain, grief, and sadness? I struggled with this question. I couldn't believe that I would *plan* to be an alcoholic, to have fibromyalgia, or to have narcissistic abusive men in my life. After I wrestled with these ideas, I found a certain sense of peace. I started to remember that I came here to learn and teach others what I learn by experience. I always knew I had a heart to help as many people as I could.

Through Reiki, I learned about energy and about vibration and frequency. In physics we learn that we are all just molecules vibrating around. Reiki is all about quantum physics! Our vibration fluctuates daily according to our emotional and physical state. When we are low vibrating, we are in lower vibrating energies with emotions such as anger, greed, depression and addiction. When we are high vibrating, we are in the vibration of love, joy, peace, understanding, and contentment. This gave me encouragement that I had some control over how I felt each day.

During my growth and healing process, it became obvious that my thoughts controlled how I felt. I realized I could choose how I thought each day and what I was going to think about. I noticed that most of my thoughts were negative and fearful. I learned that we each have 60,000 thoughts a day, and maybe more if we are overthinkers. There is no way we can consciously process 60,000 thoughts a day, but we know that we can put our thoughts in order. We order our day, for example, when we wake up, then we brush our teeth, get our coffee, and go to work or school. We have just ordered our thoughts to the most important things of the day. That shows me that we can choose what we think about, so why not choose the positive things, the hopeful things, and the happy things? If we have a choice of what to think about, let's choose well.

We each have two voices in our head every day, our ego and our higher intuitive self. The ego tends to want to protect us by having us think about the worst-case scenario. We need the ego, and that is why we have it. The ego is a necessary part of how we live in a physical body. It lets us know where we end and another person begins, and it is where we get our sense of self and our self-awareness. Our ego helps us understand who we are as unique individuals. In heaven where we come from, we are all connected as one. Our ego is a part of our "soul signature". Over the years, I have wanted to kill my ego, but we can't or we will lose the human form of ourselves. Remember, we are an intelligent design, made with all the parts we need to live a physical life.

Over time however, I came to understand that my ego really had very few constructive things to say. On the other hand, my higher self, which is my intuition or my divine team and angels, always has positive and life-giving thoughts for me. I am kind of a black-and-white person, so I decided just to listen to my higher self and ignore my ego talking. After all, it's my choice because it's my life. I do not have to think about every thought my mind produces. I can choose to let the unhelpful thoughts go. Doing so keeps me in a high vibration, out of depression and anxiety and in the place of peace and joy.

An added bonus here is that my angels and guides know everything that's going on, even my future. My divine team sees things I cannot see, and they are out for my best and highest good. Why not listen to them exclusively? Ordering my thoughts this way has helped me become a more positive, confident, and successful person. The best part is that my life became amazing and so much more enjoyable. Managing my thoughts gives me power over my vibration and keeps me in a higher vibration more consistently. I don't want to bash the ego, but start noticing what it is saying and decide whether you will listen or not. The ego keeps so many people from ever stepping out of their comfort zone in life. The ego can keep you fearful and cause you to play it safe—not what we were called here to do! In fact, if you don't learn things here and go through the hard times, you may have to come back again in order to learn the lessons. I am not sure I want to come back again. I am living my life big now, and I encourage you to. Our angels and divine team are protecting and guiding us, so you can cast aside fear and step into the lightwork you came here to do. You are supported fully by your team and by the Universe.

One difficult thing about being a lightworker is that we are extra sensitive to the energies and emotions of the world and other people. For this reason, we need to start protecting ourselves when it comes to what we hear on the news and on social media. We don't want to keep our heads in the sand about the struggles and awful things in this world, but it can hurt our soul if we can't handle it and don't limit our exposure. The best way you can help this world is to keep your vibration high and help other people. When you heal yourselves and help others, you heal the entire world. The ripple effect of the vibration of love spreads out to all the people on earth. It is far more powerful to stay in this loving state, as it continues to raise the vibration of the world and in so doing changes everything. Feeling awful, sad, and depressed about the horrible things happening today does not contribute to the healing unless you find ways to help. Sending love out is a wonderful way to change things for the better. We can do this by helping one person at a time, because we are all connected!

In order to heal yourself, you need to love yourself unconditionally. You are perfect now without changing anything. If you can love yourself and others, you are doing more healing for this world than you will ever see. The ripple effect of your love goes to every corner of the earth and heals it. It is better to pray, meditate, and continue to heal others, by which you are healing the world in a huge way, than to be depressed and down. If your vibration is low because of all the atrocities, raise it by helping in some way!

Being a lightworker requires you to take care of yourself and your energy. We can protect our energy by staying grounded and keeping ourselves healthy—eating well, sleeping well, getting moderate enjoyable exercise, and being in the state of love. Your first priority should be yourself because you cannot help others unless you are doing well. When you are healthy, you are overflowing with energy and can pour it out onto other people. When you are not healthy mentally and physically, or when you are tired and overworked, you have nothing left for others. Start putting yourself first to make sure your energy is managed. Then your light work will be more effective, and you will be a happy, healthy lightworker.

I am excited for your journey. There is so much to learn. The basis of all light work is energy; in fact, the basis of life is energy. Light is energy, and energy is light. Make sure you are studying energy while you are studying all the different ways to be a lightworker. Learning about energy helps you manage and protect your limited supply, so that you can keep your energy high and do the best lightwork you can do. I am so happy that I get to be a step on your path to being a lightworker! The truth is that you will always feel that you are missing something if you don't step into your role as lightworker. You came to be on the front lines to make the world a better place. You are a warrior for light! Find your light, and see how it wants to shine, then let it shine. Embrace how special you are and how powerful. Your priorities as a lightworker should always stay in order: you first, your family next—we do need to take care of our loved ones, as they are our soul team.Then we have to support our life with work, and here we can do lightwork. Then we do our superhero stuff. We need to be balanced lightworkers to be the most effective.

2

HEAL THYSELF

If you are ready to embark on your healer journey, you must first start to heal yourself. Some of you have already been doing this, and it is important work. Healing requires us to take a look at why we do what we do and think what we think. I used to think I had to get "rid" of my trauma in order to heal, but this is not true. Our trauma and pain have made us who we are today. It is in our cells; we cannot extricate it and toss it away. What we can do is listen to it, process it, and be willing to release it—not cast it off but relegate it to a back corner of the attic of our mind, where it loses its power and is rarely thought about. It is always our choice to take our power back from those who took it. In most cases, we did not deserve what happened to us, and it should not have happened. We reserve the right to release its power over us.

For most of my life, I carried the pain of my childhood. I did not have a horrible childhood, but it was marked by emotional abuse from the two father figures I had.T his abuse caused me to look for love and attention from boyfriends. It led me to a place of extremely low self-esteem, and I ended up marrying a narcissist. Because my father figures were narcissistic, I only knew how to be treated abusively. It was all I had ever experienced, so I chose what was familiar. I had a sweet boyfriend whom I left high and dry because I thought he was "too nice." I see so clearly now that I thought I deserved abuse and that I did not feel important enough to deserve better. Luckily that boy who was "too nice" was still single when the narcissist husband left me and my nine-month-old son for someone else. I had a second chance at a beautiful life where I could be treasured. However, it took years to reprogram my mind from my lack of self-reverence, which had turned into a lifetime of people-pleasing and self-medicating.

Even with a beautiful marriage, I still had to heal. I abused alcohol, which delayed my growth and evolution. I needed outpatient mental health services and therapy. I had to release that heavy baggage I carried around—it just needed to be cut loose. Despite being unhealed, I started my spiritual path. That is when I fully began the healing.

I learned energy healing and other spiritual concepts. I developed boundaries and slowly and consistently started to honor myself. I got sober, and my healing accelerated quickly. I started to feel good enough to heal others. I saw my family start to heal as I was healing. Notice that I did not wait until I was fully healed to start helping others. Helping others helped heal me. We will always be healing as long as we are alive. I began seeing that I had built a story about myself that was not me—it was just my difficult experiences. I realized I could let it go. But in order to let it go, I had to forgive, not for the people who hurt me but for me!

Forgiveness does not absolve what others did to us. It just declares that we are done being hurt by the same thing over and over. We don't have to carry it anymore; we can let it go. We may remember it from time to time, but it loses its power over us. These situations no longer deserve our time and attention because we are done learning from them.

Because I work with angels, I asked Archangel Michael to cut the cords attaching me to the painful experiences. Archangel Michael has a sword and can cut these negative cords that are draining us or keeping us attached to pain. We did not ask for this pain, so we reserve the right not to allow it anymore. We can be done with it. Just as when we learned that we can choose which thoughts we think, we can choose not to think about painful events anymore, and when they do come back into our mind, we can shoo them away or ask our angels to help remove them.

I struggled with forgiveness. I would think I had forgiven someone but would find myself thinking about the situation over and over.One day when I was in the bathtub, one of my favorite places for letting go of the world,, I asked my divine team how to really forgive. They told me to say this: "I forgive you. You did the best you could with the awareness you had." This made sense—the people who hurt me had very little awareness, as narcissists are unable to see how they hurt others and cannot imagine being the bad guy. They would never admit they hurt me, so why was I needing them to? I had to forgive them in order to free myself.

I continued to say this forgiveness mantra every time I

thought about the pain. I must have said it twelve times a day at the beginning. Over some weeks, I noticed I wasn't thinking about that pain or those people anymore. They had lost their power over me. I had actually forgiven them! I would go on using this forgiveness mantra with my own self, forgiving myself for past behaviors: "I did the best I could with the awareness I had." It changed everything.

I now "forgive as I go" so that trauma and pain cannot collect like a full suitcase. I have cut off my baggage through forgiveness. My past pain has dissipated in the light of forgiveness. This is not to say that we don't acknowledge things as they happen. It is important to listen to our emotions. I always treat my feelings with compassion. When I feel sad, I ask for sadness to come into my home. I give sadness a comfortable seat and offer it a cup of tea. I listen to what my sadness is telling me, I listen until the sadness is done talking, and then I hug the sadness. When it has been cared for and I am sure it is healed, I let it out the back door with love. I honor all my feelings now, and as a result, they are able to flow through my home, healed and released.

So make sure you do not spiritually bypass your feelings. Each one is teaching you something. Self-medicating or numbing just delays healing. When we don't work through our pain, it is as if we are holding inflatable balls underwater. We can keep trying to keep them from popping up, but eventually we won't be able to hold them down any longer. Sometimes they all pop up at once, and we need extra help from inpatient or outpatient mental health programs. I was helped immensely in this way. At my outpatient program, I learned cognitive behavioral therapy, which helped me manage my thoughts. I am forever grateful to that program. At times we may experience chemical imbalances, such as low serotonin, and may need antidepressant medicines. This is good, because when our brain needs help, we must help it. You would not avoid taking insulin for your diabetes if you had it. When your brain is sick, it may need meds. Just make sure you continue the healing through therapies, such as talk therapy or group therapy.

I found that as I did Reiki on clients, they would inevitably be going through something I had just worked on, and I could relay my experience with my healing. In fact, I see now that if I'd had an easy life, I could not have helped people with their problems. Since so many of my clients are empaths, I can help them go from being disempowered empaths to empowered empaths. An empowered empath makes for an incredible lightworker! When we take our power back and heal, we can show others the way.

There are so many ways to heal, but there are no shortcuts. Healing is a process and a marathon, not a sprint. The only way out is through. Be brave enough to go through it and come out the other side. Feel it to heal it. Western medicine provides mental health doctors and medicines. Sometimes we need healing facilities for more intense help. Energy healing, eye movement desensitization and reprocessing (EMDR), tapping, and twelve-step programs like AA can all help us work through trauma. If you have addiction issues, make sure that you find a dual diagnosis professional, "dual diagnosis" meaning that they address the mental health and addiction issues.

I have fibromyalgia, which I believe was brought on by

trauma. I have tried all the ways to get rid of this dis-ease, all the medicines, supplements, and exercises. When I began healing myself, I started healing the fibromyalgia. Then when I began doing Reiki on others, I started healing exponentially. Put yourself first now, work on your healing, love yourself along the way, and continue to help others as you heal. We need you to heal, lightworker!

3

ENERGY AND ENERGY HEALING

Energy healing is vibrational. We all vibrate at a certain frequency. When we are sick or depressed, we are usually in a lower vibration. Using drugs and alcohol is very low vibrating, as are being angry and judgmental. Conversely, being healthy and happy are very high vibrations. It is difficult to heal when we are low vibrating, and what ultimately heals us is rising to a higher vibration or full health. We know that when someone's heart stops, we can shock them with energy to restart it. In the case of mental health, when a person is unable to regain their mental health, modern electroshock therapy can be used to regain normal brain function. These are both extreme measures, but they demonstrate that we are indeed run by energy. From day to day, most of us vibrate somewhere in the middle, not too high or low. Things that make us happy raise our vibration, while stressful difficult situations lower it.

When I was in lower vibration, I did not feel good. I was depressed and physically sick. I wish I had understood energy back then; if I had, I may have been able to heal faster. We all have a certain amount of energy each day, and when we run out of that energy, we need to sleep. When we are sick or low vibrating, we have less energy to draw from and need to rest more. Unfortunately, most people are overworked and don't give themselves the rest they need to restore their energy. They may be borrowing from tomorrow's energy supply to get through today, causing a constant energy deficit. You may notice that even when you get enough hours of sleep, you are still tired. Americans put such an emphasis on busyness that we are a country of exhausted, stressed, sick people. This needs to stop.

Most of my clients come to me as a last resort. They are already in a bad energetic place when they come for healing. I do a lot of crisis Reiki, which is needed when people are at the point of a mental or physical breakdown. Reiki and sound healing are both vibratory healing modalities and are very effective. All my clients leave in a higher vibration than when they came. This has nothing to do with me, and everything to do with God/Source energy and their divine team. As a Reiki practitioner, I channel universal life force energy through myself to my client. It would not be good to use my own energy to heal others, and I don't have to when I am connected to Source. Using my energy would drain me of the energy I need and would depend on my vibration at the time. This universal life force energy, or chi, is intuitive and knows what my client needs. When I am done with a session, I know my client has gotten what they need.

Reiki and other energy healing modalities are great ways to learn how to channel energy. We are all connected to God/Source and can tap into that energy, but we need to learn how. Reiki and energy healing teach us how to be a channel to funnel healing energy to others from the Source of all love and healing. In acupuncture, a practitioner works by unblocking chi energy with needles. A counselor or therapist helps to unblock negative energy by listening and guiding us to realize what is causing our pain. Sound healing works through the vibration that causes sound, and the vibration of sound is very healing. I use hands-on healing to bring energetic balance back to the chakras or energy centers of the body.

We have seven major chakras, which are like a battery in a car. Sometimes our battery dies and needs a jump. The chakras can be in slow vibration, which makes it harder for our body to stay in homeostasis. Our body is constantly healing itself. When we get a cut, our body rushes in to stop the bleeding and heal it. Homeostasis is our optimal state of health, and our body works constantly to stay in homeostasis. Our cells are in a constant state of regeneration. When you receive Reiki, you balance or restart your chakras. When your chakras are back online energetically, you can heal yourself. In terms of energy, Reiki is a "hand up off the ground." If you go back to what was draining your energy in the first place, you will drain your battery. I always advise my clients to look at the things that brought them to me. What caused the imbalance? I recommend that they change things in their life that are low vibrating and add things that add to their vibration.

Some things that drain us are struggling relationships, jobs that are too demanding and don't bring us joy, and unhealthy habits. Your body needs proper fuel and energy management. Things that give us energy are loving relationships, work we enjoy that gives us purpose, and high vibration foods like fruits, vegetables, and water. In order to maintain a good frequency or vibration, we need to take care of ourselves. In what areas of life are you not taking the best care? What are you allowing that brings your vibration down? We don't have much control in life, but certain things we can control. Protecting our energy is something important that we can do. Before getting to a place of crisis, we can notice red flags such as illness and exhaustion and then engage in serious self-care. Before our batteries die, we can give ourselves what we need to continue running well.

Take an inventory of your energy every day, and take care of yourself first. When you are ready, decide what healing modality you want to try and learn it. There are so many different schools of Reiki. The original is Usui Reiki, but others include Karuna Reiki, angel Reiki, and energy healing techniques such as Integrated Energy Therapy (IET). Divination tools like tarot and oracle card reading are a form of energy healing. Mediumship is a powerful form of energy healing because you are helping people with their grief by connecting them to their loved one in spirit. Some healers perform past life regression sessions or read the akashic records. Sound healing with instruments is an amazing healing technique. There are so many amazing ways to heal with energy. Do some research to find what lights up your soul, and learn it!

Sometimes practitioners study with a mentor or guru. I am all for that, as long as that person wants you to graduate eventually. Beware the teacher who keeps you paying them after you have learned the lesson. Don't work with anyone who is ego-driven and imparts the feeling that they are more knowledgeable or powerful .No one in a physical body has it all figured out, believe me. I want you to know that you are totally capable and perfectly equipped to become an energy healer. There is a pervasive idea that healers are born with special gifts, and that is true, but *we are all born with those gifts*. Energy healers and lightworkers have just chosen to strengthen and develop their gifts, and you can too. Be careful of teachers who are charging extremely large amounts of money for their teachings. We need to charge for our services, but there are limits—people should not go broke in order to learn lightwork. You do not need to cause yourself financial distress by paying for classes. There are so many things to learn, and you can't learn everything all at once, although you may want to.

What are these gifts we are born with? Not everyone is born with the gift of compassion and empathy, so that is one of the greatest gifts you have as a lightworker. You are able to help people solely with that gift. We were all also given the "clairs" as gifts: clairvoyance, clairaudience, clairsentience, and claircognizance. I believe we have all these, but each of us differs in which we are better at. Let's start with clairvoyance or clear seeing. If you see or can imagine pictures in your mind, you may have this gift. Clairvoyants can see angels or people who have passed, and they can use this gift of clear seeing to help others. Clairaudience is clear hearing, which is my strongest gift. I hear angels and guides and relay those messages to people who need them. I sometimes hear people in spirit even though I don't have a strong mediumship gift (maybe I will work on this one at some point). Clairsentience is a clear feeling. You can feel energies or entities around you, and you may feel others' feelings as well. Clariscognizance is clear knowing—you just know, or you have a knowing. Claircognizance is my other gift and my daughter's main gift. We just know things.

Which of these do you have? If any sound familiar, those are probably the ones because your angels are giving you those thoughts.

Learn about the different gifts, and start practicing yours. No one automatically knows how to do something. You have to learn it. You need to learn and practice your gifts to become a master of them. The more we dedicate ourselves to learning, the faster and stronger our gifts will become. It is exciting, so look for healers with your gifts and learn from them. They were once new and unskilled, but they honed these gifts in order to make a difference in people's lives.

While you learn, stay connected to your team. They will help you with the learning process and guide you to the next step on the spiritual path. I use many different tools in my Reiki sessions, including crystals, oracle cards, sound healing, and automatic writing. This last tool is a way to get messages from your angels and guides that I learned over the last few years. I am clairaudient, so the angels talk to me during my sessions. I noticed that they would start talking to me about a client on the morning of their appointment, and an hour later they were practically talking my ear off. So as not to forget the messages they were giving me, I started automatic writing before the client arrived. The writing is always on point and helps me with the first session because I may not know anything about the person beforehand. I put the paper behind me, and bring it out to read during our initial conversation.

To practice automatic writing, simply get in a quiet place with a pen and paper. It helps to meditate or center yourself and quiet your mind. Put the pen to the paper and wait for a word or thought. It may start slowly, and then gradually the angels and guides will give you more words. Over time, when they see that you are listening to them, they will give you information more rapidly. Sometimes my hand cramps up because I am writing so fast. This is a beautiful way for the angels to show their person that they are there and know what you are going through.

Try different ways to use energy and vibration to heal. Choose the things that resonate for you. Over time you will find many ways to connect to God/Source and your divine team. When our information comes from Source and angels, it is coming from the highest vibration of love and is for our highest good.

The most important lightwork I have ever done is to raise my children. I made so many mistakes and wasn't always the best at it, but I loved them so much, and I wanted them to have a good childhood. I can say I tried harder at that than anything else in my life and still was not perfect. You see, we can't be perfect—we are human and make mistakes, and we have regrets even when we do our best. To parents, grandparents, great-grandparents, aunts and uncles, know that you are contributing to the growth of the next generations. This will do more for the world than any other thing. Honestly, kindness and love are the greatest things we can do as lightworkers. Think of all the lightworkers in the world. The one who smiles and speaks to the homeless person or addict is the most powerful lightworker. Think about that.

ENERGY HEALING SESSIONS
AND ANGEL MESSAGES

I have been doing Reiki for twenty years. The first ten or so years, I did not believe in myself. I felt like an imposter, even though my clients seemed to be helped by their time with me. I made sure the lights were low, and the music soft. I had the candles and incense burning and spent lots of time with each person. If you were to look at my sessions from the outside, they would look wonderful, but inside I lacked faith in myself and by default in the Reiki as well. Oh, I knew that Reiki worked and was very powerful when others did it, but I doubted that I had the ability to do it. Even when clients told of the colors they saw and the things they felt, I wasn't sure. If I knew then what I know now, my Reiki practice would have grown quickly.

If you only take one thing from this book, let it be this.

You have everything you need to be a healer because
you are directly connected to God/Source, and that
power is for you to use here!

No other person is more connected or has more magic than you. They may have practiced more, but they don't have any more power available to them than you do. If you go into your Reiki or other lightwork knowing and truly believing this, you will be able to channel that healing energy immediately. After all, you have been healing others most of your life. Each time you helped or cared for someone, you offered healing. Think about a world where each person realizes and uses their power to heal and raise the vibration here on earth. Begin where you are, do what you can, and heal as you go.

I would like at this point to share some of my incredible sessions and some of the gngel wisdom from them. Your healing may look different from mine, and that is as it should be. We are all here to offer our own special gifts and to share our soul signature. People need what you have. Source will send you the people—you just have to believe in your ability and your magic.

The first client I remember was not a great experience, but it taught me a lesson. This man was a skeptic and a client from my thirty-five years as a hairdresser. I finished his haircut and in my excitement started explaining this Reiki class I had just taken.

"Well, why don't you do it on me?'" he asked.

I had some hesitation, but I agreed and had him lie on my couch. I started giving Reiki, concentrating on the steps

I learned and feeling pretty good. When I was done, he immediately said, "I didn't feel a thing." This ruined Reiki for me right when I should have been looking forward to my future in energy healing. I decided at that moment that I didn't have "it," and I kept that doubt for years after. From that, however, I learned that I should never take a client who is a skeptic because their higher self will probably not accept the healing anyway. I wish I hadn't been so quick to believe a man who was very negative in the first place. Now I only take clients who call me to set up an appointment and then keep the appointment, which tells me they already believe and are ready to accept the healing energy of Reiki.

When I first started giving angel messages, I must have really impressed a client because she began sending her whole family to me. She had a huge family and also sent one of her friends. The woman was very shy and barely spoke. I kept asking questions to get her to open up, but she would not budge. I even asked her outright if she had any questions for her angels.

"No!" she replied.

No? Who doesn't want to hear from angels?! Then I realized I was not hearing her angels anyway, so I cut the conversation short and began the Reiki session. She seemed to relax, though not fully, and when I was done, I wasn't sure she had gotten anything out of it.

After she left, I asked her angels why they were not talking to me on her behalf. They said it was because she wouldn't allow them to. Our angels have to honor our free will, and the client had not given them permission to talk to me—she had remained closed. She did not even realize it. She was just an extremely private person and did not feel comfortable being vulnerable. I do see that with clients who have post-traumatic stress disorder (PTSD) or complex post traumatic syndrome disorder (CPTSD). We need to respect and honor our clients and their comfort zone. We just ask our angels and guides to be with us and keep channeling God/Source energy. Reiki does no harm, and even if they only allow a little healing, it can be profound.

Once when a client came for his Reiki appointment, my sense was that he was under the influence of something, but I wasn't sure what. During the angel message part, I could not hear from his angels, and he was nodding off mid-sentence. As with the closed-off client, I quickly skipped to the Reiki part, and within minutes he was snoring. I was disappointed, but Reiki works while people are asleep just as well, so I finished the session. I could not get him to wake up! He kept sleeping for another hour.

I went upstairs, and my mom, who lives with me, said, "Where's your client?"

"He is sound asleep," I said, "and I can't wake him up."

When he finally woke, he claimed he felt fabulous and wanted to come back the next day. I explained that Reiki doesn't need to be done every day, and when he did come back, he couldn't be under the influence of drugs or alcohol. He sheepishly explained that he had taken Valium because of the stress he was under.

"Reiki can't really work well when you are in that state," I told him, so he agreed to be sober for our next appointment. Happily, he was.

Angels have a hard time being in the vibration of someone

on drugs or alcohol. Those substances are very low vibrating, and the angels have a hard time lowering their vibration to that level. This is why we should never give Reiki or energy healing while under the influence of mind-altering substances ourselves. The exception is plant medicine like cannabis or psilocybin, and even then it needs to be a lighter dose.

My favorite clients to work with are the ones struggling with addiction. That may seem weird, but addiction is my comfort zone. I understand it. I know people can find recovery from their addiction, because if I can get sober, you can too. I have been in recovery for seven years, and I have found some pretty effective ways to stay sober with energy healing.

One client who was referred to me for Reiki had recently gotten out of rehab for a drug addiction and had also lost her mother. I had not met her before, but I could feel the pain as soon as she arrived, so we dug in quickly. The conversation flowed between us, and the angels chimed in with their amazing guidance. When it came time to do the Reiki part of the session, I got her comfortable on my massage table and began. As soon as I placed my hands on her, she started wailing. Her cries were guttural, and she was lifting off the massage table. I was a little freaked out, to be honest. I had often had people cry on my Reiki table, but nothing like this. I asked my angels and guides if this was something I should be worried about. Was this a demon or lower-vibrating entity or energy?

The Angels quickly answered me: *It's pain!* They told me to keep my hands on her and let her cry. With this assurance, I did keep my hands on her and became a clear channel so that the power of universal life force energy from God/Source could come through and give her what she needed for healing. The session went on for about forty minutes. After about half an hour, her cries grew softer, but the tears still flowed from her eyes. When I was done, I gently brought her back to the room, and we just looked at each other. We hugged. Not the soft hug I normally give my clients, but a grasping and holding-on-for-dear-life hug. She thanked me profusely, and I thanked her for giving me the chance to help her heal this immense pain. I earned my angel wings that day, and from then on I had no fear of even the worst pain. In fact, I say to the Universe, "Bring it!" I am always protected by my team. Those intense healings are some of my favorites.

Now that I have shared some of my more challenging Reiki sessions, let's talk about some that were uplifting and life-changing.

I first started doing Reiki in the basement of my home, where it was dark and somewhat noisy, with everyone walking around above us in the kitchen. When we were able to buy a new home, my first priority was a quiet, beautiful place to do Reiki and energy healing. We had a Realtor looking for the perfect lake house for us to live in. My husband loves boating and water skiing, and I love the water.

During this house-hunting period of my life, I had just finished giving a Reiki class in which we wrote down our wishes and dreams and put them into a Reiki box, just a simple wooden box given to me by my Reiki teacher. Immediately after the class, I turned on my phone and saw a house pop up on Zillow. It was just off the lake on an inlet, but it was a small ranch and we needed a bigger home. We needed two master bedrooms, one for my husband and me, and one for my parents. We also needed space for our youngest son. My Realtor would never have shown me this home because it didn't have what we said we needed. Since I had just asked my angels for the perfect home, I knew they were guiding me to go see it. I quickly called the Realtor, who lived in the neighborhood on the lake, and arranged to view it.

Before we left, I showed my husband the listing, and he didn't even want to go look at it. The home was extremely outdated and small, but it had a beautiful sunroom overlooking a nice-size backyard and the lake. As soon as we arrived, I knew this was our home. My husband and son were looking at me like I was crazy, but I just knew that this was the house for us. I explained to everyone that I watch a lot of HGTV, so I could see the possibilities of it being a great house.

When we arrived at the house, I was happy to see that our Realtor had her husband, a builder, with her. I was able to ask him questions about remodeling the house and he told us that we could. I don't believe we would have bought the house if a builder had not been there. Was that a blessing from the angels or what? Even though my husband and son could not see the possibilities in this house, I knew it was the home for us. The Angels had given it to us. It was during a time when houses were selling quickly for more money than the asking price, so I knew we had to make a quick decision. The Realtor encouraged us to put in an offer for more money than the listing price. Since nothing was going to change my mind about this house, we put an offer in for more than it was worth. They were taking offers for the next twenty-four hours, so we had to wait to see whether our offer was accepted. More than thirty potential buyers put in an offer on the house, despite the shape it was in.

After we got home, anxiety set in. I started doubting whether angels could be experts on buying a house on earth. Fear swirled in my head about the huge amount of work it would take to remodel the house, and how much that would cost. Then I reminded myself that I live my life trusting my angels for everything, and I talk to them all day long. If the house was meant to be ours, the angels would make it happen. If our offer was accepted, it was meant to be.

The next night at 8 p.m., my Realtor called to congratulate us. Our offer had been accepted. This is how the angels work for me in my life, and they will do this for you too if you ask them for help and guidance.

I was so excited to start seeing clients in my new Reiki room!. The way the sun comes in and fills the room with light is so beautiful, and the nature outside is very powerful. Clients who come to my home sometimes start crying as soon as they walk in the door. This is the effect the angels have on people, and my house is always full of angels.

Before I start a Reiki session, I ask my client's angels and my angels to come. I protect my space by asking Archangel Michael to come in, and I protect myself with the white light of energy from Source. Before my clients arrive, I usually do automatic writing for them. To start, I take some deep breaths, close my eyes, and come back to center. This meditative state is perfect for hearing angels. I explain it as an extended non-thinking pause. I am emptying my mind of my own thoughts and waiting to hear the thoughts of the angels and guides.

These messages drop into my head, and it would be easy to confuse them with my own thoughts, but I did not actively think about them. Then I begin writing.

When the client arrives, I offer tea or water and ask them to sit on my pink couch, where we start discussing anything they feel comfortable talking about. The tears sometimes start flowing right away because my clients come with such pain and struggle.

I am committed to going into the deep trenches of pain with my clients and pulling them back into the light. There are times when a client takes a while to trust me, and I understand. I always take the time we need. I book only one or two clients a day for this very reason. Conversation with the angels can sometimes take one to two hours. There must be some sort of time vortex in my Reiki room, because the time seems to fly when I am with my clients, and they agree with this perception. It's almost as if time stands still in honor of the healing process.

This work is not for everyone, but if you are a lightworker, it may be for you. It is such an honor to meet people at their worst time and at their lowest vibration, and then channel universal life force energy and angel messages in order to bring their energy back into a high vibration.

The angels are very expedient and get right to the point, allowing for little small talk. We tend to tackle the big issues quickly. Angels are serious but also have a very funny sense of humor. Since I am not extremely clairvoyant, I do not see the angels. I am clairaudient, so I hear them. I have been arguing with them about letting me see them, and they tell me I am too distractible and if they show themselves I will not be able to do the work I am supposed to do.

I ask them who they are, what their names are, and what they look like. They always tell me that it doesn't matter; they are simply energy beings of light. I often picture them as we humans do, as having wings and flowing a white gown with light emanating around them. After reading Sonya Choquette's book *Ask Your Guides*, I asked my angels, "How shall I address you?" They answered by telling me that I had an angel named Patience, because I don't have any patience and I need the angel to help me be patient. I felt their energy sort of laughing at me, and I laughed too. The truth is, I don't have any patience! So I'm glad I have an angel called Patience to help me do the work. There were three other angels who together were named Emmanuel, which means "God with us." I thought that was just beautiful. I am sure that I also have Jesus and Kuan Yin, a bodhisattva, on my divine team. A bodhisattva is a compassionate healer.

I may never see these angels, but I trust completely that they are there. I hear them and I know that they are committed to helping me with my Reiki sessions and angel messages. My clients' angels love them so much that I sometimes feel moved to tears, the love coming from their angels is so incredible. I try to convey that love to the person while they are on my couch and on my massage table. Everyone needs to know how loved they are. Since my clients' angels know them so well and know the mission they are here to accomplish, they have a lot to say. When I am speaking to the angels, I feel when they are intense and when they are light and jovial. Either way, their vibration is very high and energizes me and keeps me focused.

Mediumship is not a strong gift for me yet, so I don't ever offer to connect with my clients' loved ones in spirit. When I am asked by my clients if I can connect to their loved one, I usually just say I am not good at that. There have been times, however, when people in spirit have shown up to my Reiki sessions. One of my clients was in grief over losing her father, and she was also in a bad romantic relationship. This boyfriend of hers actually poured an entire bottle of water over her head during a fight. I try not to let my own opinions and triggers come into play during my Reiki sessions, but in this case when she asked me what her father thought of this man, he jumped right in and said, *He is not good enough for her.* It happened so quickly that I was not even able to stop it from coming out of my mouth. I believe it was a message her father in spirit really needed her to hear. Some people hear angel messages that make them think about leaving a partner but override their intuition out of fear. My goal with my clients is to give them back their power and to remind them of who they are and how much they deserve. It is not my job nor the angels' job to tell a person to get out of a relationship or marriage. It is only our job to build the self-esteem and integrity of our clients. It is important that we remain objective even when we have human opinions. The angels don't tell us what to do, and they never will. They only give suggestions and allow us to have free will in our lives.

Another client of mine had lost her mother just a year before her Reiki session. After we spoke and finished her

Reiki session, she looked at me from the massage table and asked if I could get a message from her mother. I told her I was not good at mediumship, but I asked her what she would ask her mother.

"I would ask her if I should start this new company on my own," she said. She was starting a new counseling practice but was afraid she would fail.

Her mom immediately stepped in. "My daughter can do anything. She can do this."

My client said that was exactly what her mother would have said, and she left feeling encouraged. Angels want each of us to cast fear aside in order to live our fullest life, and they are behind us supporting everything we do.

For a time I seemed to have clients who had lost a child. This is the strongest grief I have ever experienced during Reiki sessions. I cannot imagine losing a child, and a parent should never have to go through this. I was surprised at how incredibly positive these clients were. I was humbled to see such joy in the midst of such incredible pain. Angels give me the impression that they are working overtime for people who are grieving in order to keep them safe. Angels are close to those who are grieving. If you have lost someone you love, the angels are with you, wrapping their wings around you. I hope that you can feel that.

Sometimes we just have to sit with our clients along with their pain. At times there are no words; nothing can be said to lessen the grief. Those are the times my angels ask me to pause and just accompany my client where they are. I often tell my client I am sorry and I wish they didn't have to go through this pain. We never get over losing someone; we just learn to live with their absence, and we can look forward to seeing them again. For our loved ones on the other side of spirit, there is no sense of time. They will see us tomorrow, even if it is decades until we pass. Our loved ones are in their highest state of joy and love on the other side, and we don't have to worry about them. In fact, it is they who are worried about us, and they are with us all closely through our lives, helping us and loving us.

I often use oracle cards when I work with clients. I have certain decks I love to work with. My favorite is a Quan Yin oracle deck, and I believe it is for lightworkers. We usually talk with the angels, and then after we've had our talk, we pick a card. I cannot tell you how incredible it is when the card they pick speaks directly to what we have just talked about. My belief in using oracle cards to give my clients messages has grown exponentially. It is just another way to give messages to our clients from their divine team and from Source. One of my favorite decks is an angel card deck by Kyle Gray. If angels resonate with you, I encourage you to look into Kyle Gray and Sonya Choquette, both angel intuitives who have taught me so much.

My first Reiki teacher was an angel intuitive, but I had no interest in angels then—they had never been on my radar. Ten years later, the angels started speaking to me too. There are truly no accidents in the world of energy healing. We are always sent the right teachers and the right clients. I don't advertise. There are no accidents when my clients find me because it's based on referrals. One person comes and has a beautiful experience, and they refer their loved ones and friends to me. As a result, I have a constant stream of Reiki clients, the perfect number for me.

I had a client I had never met coming for a Reiki session. She had attended one of my Reiki Restorative classes. In my Reiki restorative class, I balance my students' chakras while they are in a restorative yoga pose. At the end of these classes, my husband, Joe, does sound healing. Reiki restoratives are always very powerful, and a restorative class is one of my favorite ways to give Reiki. This beautiful client called afterward to get a Reiki appointment with me at my home.

Before she came, I began automatic writing, which left no doubt that she either wanted to get pregnant or needed to give birth to something in her life. From the words of the angels, I was steering toward an actual pregnancy. Since I didn't know anything about this woman, I just finished my automatic writing and put it behind me. Automatic writing is always spot on, but because I doubt myself, I don't put it out right away—I wait until I have spoken to my client for a while.

When this client sat down, tears immediately started flowing from her eyes. There was no small talk; we got right to the point. Her biggest wish was to have a baby with her wonderful husband, but she was struggling to get pregnant. Her life was otherwise wonderful, and she had everything she wanted except a child. The hair on my arms stood up as soon as she spoke, because that is what the angels had told me before she came. After we discussed her struggle to conceive, I read to her what the angels had given me in the automatic writing, and she was blown away that I had written this before she came. How did I know? I told her that I didn't have to know because the angels know. Then we chose a card out of a beautiful deck that I have, and the card said *sacred birth*. We were so encouraged that her card was about giving birth. I continue to send her Reiki and love on her IVF journey, and I know she will be an amazing mother.

5

WHAT ENERGY HEALING CAN LOOK LIKE

Every single angel message and Reiki session I give surprises me. Angels always come through loud and clear, and the healing energy of Source flows through powerfully. This powerful energy healing has nothing to do with me; there is no pressure on me.

Among the thousands of healers in this world, most have the heart to truly help people, but be aware that some can be focused on the financial aspects of healing. In my practice, I do charge for my time, and I may spend as long as four hours with a client. That being said, I sometimes barter services or take gifts, and if someone can't afford Reiki, I do it for free or for an energy transfer of some kind. We will not leave here with any of our things; we leave with a record of how we cared for others. While we are here, we need money to survive, and so we are compensated for our time and the skills we have worked hard to perfect.

Now let's talk about actual steps to giving energy healing so you can see if it is something you would like to learn.

I am a practitioner and teacher of Reiki and integrated energy therapy (IET). There are hundreds of schools of Reiki, and a million different ways to do energy healing, but I will give examples of how my sessions look. Before my client gets to my house, I make time to meditate, breathe, and come back to center. Next I do automatic writing because my angels usually are communicating to me already about the client. I clear my space with incense, and ask Archangel Michael to come and protect the space and my Reiki session. I use the Reiki power symbol on all four corners of the room and on myself. Have everything you need for the session available. It's important that you hold space during the whole session, and you don't want to be searching for things or leaving the room while you have your client.

When I start my Reiki session, I get the client comfortable on my massage table. I ask that they remove their shoes, if they are comfortable with that. I offer a bolster for under the knees and pillows for under the head. A blanket is nice and comfy, but the client may get hot and decline it. I place my hands over the client's ears and hold this position to build rapport and establish the connection of our energies. I will stay here for a minute or two. While here, I take a deep breath and come back to my center, then I envision placing myself outside my body. Now I am a clear channel for universal life force energy, which knows what my client needs. I don't know what they need, but God does. By becoming a clear channel for Source, I can be sure that my client gets exactly what they need for their highest healing. .

The next step is cutting cords with Archangel Michael, the angel with the sword who is spoken about in many religious texts. Michael is the angel of protection. I use a selenite sword as a symbolic tool. The real work is done by Michael. I ask that he cut any cords that are draining my client for their highest good. Archangel Michael will only cut cords that my client's higher self agrees to. Even though some cords need to be cut, the client might not be ready to cut them. Angels never impose their own will on us but give us free will at all times. They respect and honor our healing process. They are always willing to step in and help when we are ready. I move the sword over the client in an infinity shape and blow away the cords that were cut.

To start the Reiki, you have a couple choices. Some practitioners start at the root chakra, and others at the crown. Either way is good. I start at the root by hovering my hands over the root but not actually touching the client. The root is at the base of the spine and is a private area that we should not be touching. Next I move up to the sacral chakra. Here I lay my hands side by side. On men, I avoid getting my hands anywhere close to the belt for privacy. I will keep my hands on this area for as long as needed, trusting my intuition about when to move on. While laying my hands on the client, I imagine tapping into the power of the Universe, and the universal life force energy comes down through my crown and out through my hands. For a long time when I first started doing Reiki, I would repeat the Reiki symbols three times silently. (I cannot share the symbols here because you need to get an attunement to use them.) I continue up by holding my hands on the remaining chakras, the solar plexus, heart, throat, third eye, and crown chakras.

I now incorporate the IET healing modality, which engages the client to participate actively in the release of emotional imbalances. I speak gently, asking them to release and then inviting them to imprint a healing option. Reiki is generally done with no words from the practitioner, just the healing flow of energy. IET is a quiet exchange of healing suggestions. These two modalities work well together. When I am done, I may feel compelled by intuition to go back to certain areas and spend time there. I finish by sweeping all the old energy down their arms and legs and out through the feet. Then I gently ask the person to gather back their parts and come back to the space. I instruct them to take some deep breaths and wiggle their fingers and toes, inviting movement back to their body. Every energy healing will look different because I trust my intuition to guide me to the places I need to address.

I love to learn new and unique ways to do energy healing. Reiki can be done completely hands off by hovering over the chakras with your hands—the energy still reaches the client and isn't less powerful. Reiki can be sent to other places, even other countries, because energy is not bound by space or time. It is all so interesting! Massage and acupuncture are forms of energy healing, as well as homeopathic remedies. Different cultures have their energy healing traditions, for example ayahuasca ceremonies or others involving medicines such as mushrooms or peyote. There are no limits to the healing that can be done outside traditional pharmaceuticals and Western medicine. I am not against these health institutions, but I encourage people to do both energy healing and healing with a doctor. Nutrition will be the key to health either way.

Through healthy eating and watching what we put into our bodies, we will keep our energy in a higher vibration, which is best for our mind, body, and spirit connection.

I also incorporate sound healing into my energy healing sessions. There is no quicker way to balance someone's energy than listening to sound. Sound is vibration, and vibration is energy. I use crystal bowls, Tibetan bowls, a gong, and Koshi bells while I play. You do not need any training or any background in music to do sound healing, and you don't have to be able to read music. Start small with a bowl or two, and keep practicing. Everyone loves sound healing, even if they are not "spiritual," as sound affects every person.

After all my sessions, I give my clients aftercare instructions. It's important that they drink a lot of water. An Epsom salt or sea salt bath, if possible, will help remove any remaining lower-vibrating energies. A salt scrub in the shower works just as well. We can take on the energies of other people and of the world so a good daily practice for energy maintenance will help their newly balanced chakras stay in good shape. I call this maintenance "spiritual hygiene."

When you find the energy healing you would like to do, you will develop healing sessions that resonate with you, and you will be giving the world healing one client at a time. I am compelled to teach the world to be energy healers, if only for themselves and their families. I teach Reiki and IET, and if you like to teach, you may want to teach as well. Since you are a unique individual with special gifts, you can do it your way. It helps to get instruction and options so that you have a foundation to build on. You do not have to learn or be attuned to any form of energy healing; you are already connected to

Source energy. You can start opening up and tapping into that connection right now. Just ask your angels and guides to help you, and be open to all the ways to channel this universal energy. We are connected because we are all God/Source. It is where we came from. We are fractals here on earth of that all-knowing and loving life force energy. Every time you have touched or hugged someone, you have given them Reiki. If you have ever placed your hand on your child's forehead when they are sick, you have given Reiki.

I ask for help in all my healing sessions from angels and guides, enlisting the expertise of my client's angels. They know what they need to heal and will help assist me. I am constantly learning from the angels, and trusting everything they say makes my job easier. When I first started doing Reiki, I did not hear angels, but my Reiki was no less effective. Some people do not engage the help of their divine team, and they give powerful Reiki sessions anyway. Each lightworker has different gifts and different ways to do energy healing, and all of those are perfect. Don't ever think you have to feel energy or hear angels and guides to be a good energy healer.

When giving Reiki, my hands usually remain cold. I still know that the Reiki is flowing; I just happen to have cold hands and feet. Sometimes, as my Reiki session goes on, my hands heat up, but I never feel tingling. We all experience Reiki differently. Don't let the experiences of other people have any effect on your energy healing. You can be confident that Reiki will give your client what they need. The compassion we have attracts higher-vibrating beings. These light beings love to help us transfer energy to our clients. Never doubt that the intention of helping someone comes with an army of angels and guides and the full power of universal life force energy. Source is so happy that we are helping humanity, and this divine team will meet us and our clients. They are with us during our healing sessions and give us everything we need.

You cannot do Reiki "wrong," and you can't mess it up. First of all, Reiki can do no harm. When you are tapped into God/Source, it is always going to turn out perfectly. After learning Reiki, I worked at remembering all the steps. I felt that if I missed a step, the Reiki would not work. I laugh now when I think about that. There were so many times that I forgot to "start" the session by saying "Reiki on," "Reiki go," or "Reiki flow." I would get to the end of the session and think that I had never started it because I did not say the words. But Reiki is never dependent on any steps. It is the intention to help another which freely starts the flow of healing energy. It is all intention. I could stand with my hands on the same spot the whole time, and Reiki would flow to every place the client needs it, as long as I remember that I am not the one doing the healing and allow Source to come through me. Reiki is effective even when you give a brief session. A longer session helps the client relax into the flow of energy, but you can give a quick burst of Reiki. A little Reiki is better than none. Make sure the client is comfortable. Offer a bolster or pillow under the legs to avoid lower back strain, and have a blanket on hand in case they are cold. It is nice to tuck the blanket around their feet. Make sure the room is at a comfortable temperature and free from distractions.

Reiki can be done anywhere. You do not need to rent space to do it. I have always done Reiki from my home. Reiki is not usually a job you can count on to make enough money. It ebbs and flows with clients. Sometimes you are very busy, and other times you will experience a lull, so before you consider renting space or spending money to do energy healing, wait until you have a consistent clientele. You can do Reiki at the client's home and make house calls. I go to people's homes after they have had surgery to give Reiki because it is excellent for helping people heal. You can do Reiki on a chair or outside, anywhere. I have given Reiki on a plane, in a yoga studio, and on a lake. You don't need a designated space to give energy healing. Just have whatever tools you use nearby, such as essential oils, incense, music, or sound-healing instruments. Flexibility is wonderful. I am so excited for you to start healing the world in your own powerful way.

6

LIGHTWORKERS
CAN SAVE LIVES

Four years ago, I donated my kidney to someone I don't know. Second to raising my children, I am most proud of my decision to save someone's life by giving them one of my kidneys, in what is called an altruistic or non-directed donation. When I was doing research toward becoming a kidney donor, I learned that most empathic people have a larger amygdala, which is an almond-shaped part of the brain involved with emotions and processing experience. Studies have shown that lightworkers have a biological difference, a bigger amygdala! I watched all sorts of videos on YouTube about people who had donated their kidney and read all about kidney donation.

I had wanted to donate bone marrow since I was in high school. I signed up for the bone marrow donor list but never got a call. When I was fifty-two, I saw a post on Facebook calling for a partial liver donor. I immediately got the information and contacted Northwestern Hospital in Chicago. I needed to be a blood match and found out that I did not have the same blood type as the woman who needed a partial liver donation. I was still very interested in donating, so I filled out paperwork to donate my kidney.

Two or three months went by, and I had almost forgotten that I had filled out the application when a social worker from the transplant department called to ask whether I was still interested in donating. I told her I was, so the long process began. Month after month, I made the hour and a half drive to the city to give blood samples and urine samples. My husband and kids were less than excited at first. I got the "Are you crazy?" look and a lot of understandable resistance. If my loved one was offering to donate to someone unknown, I would be very worried too. My daughter was immediately supportive, but my oldest son was completely against it at first, and my youngest son was worried. My husband was very worried, because when I get an idea to do something, he knows I usually do it. My mom was understandably very worried. I realized I needed to get all the research together to win them over, since my first priority is my family and being around for them.

While doing my research on becoming a kidney donor, I learned that we only need one kidney, and when we donate a kidney, the other grows bigger to compensate. The lifespan of kidney donors is longer than average because you have to be in such good shape to donate. I learned that if I ever need a kidney after donating, I will be at the top of the list to receive a donation. With all this information in hand, I wrote a letter to my family about my desire to donate my kidney. They all slowly got on board and became my biggest support system.

I signed up for the journey to donation, which lasted almost eighteen months. I had to go to the hospital and give gallons of blood samples. CT scans were taken of my kidney and surrounding organs. Since I had a history of alcohol use disorder in my medical records, I was continuously blood-tested to make sure I wasn't back to drinking. The most comprehensive tests were psychological. I was asked repeatedly why I wanted to donate my kidney to a stranger. The truth is, I believe it was my angels—I had a supernatural need to save someone's life, and kidney donation was my way of doing it. But when I was asked, I simply replied, "Because I have two and only need one, and someone else deserves to live." Records from my psychiatrist were obtained, and the psychiatrist at Northwestern Hospital gave me lengthy psychological exams. Apparently, it takes a very strange person to donate their kidney to a stranger.

I was almost at the end of all the tests when I got the call saying they had matched me with someone. Was I still interested in donating? After all the tests and the time it took, my heart still wanted to save someone's life by donating my kidney. By the time surgery was scheduled, it was September 2020—the height of Covid. Because of pandemic protocols, I wouldn't be able to have anyone with me at the hospital.

They told me that I could change my mind up until the time I was wheeled into surgery, but I had made my mind up a long time ago and wasn't going to change it. My husband was nervous when he dropped me off in front of the hospital and waved goodbye. It was very hard for both of us that he wasn't allowed in with me. He had to go back to work and wait for the call that I had come out of the surgery and was okay. He was allowed to come during visiting hours, but I was extremely nauseous and encouraged him to get home and get some sleep. I was discharged the next day, and he came to pick me up.

They didn't tell me who got my kidney, only that the recipient was a woman about my age and that the kidney was shipped to Philadelphia, Pennsylvania. I signed a paper saying that the person who received my kidney could contact me. I provided my address and phone number, but she never contacted me. I knew it was possible that the person would never contact me, and I accepted that. I did not donate the kidney to be thanked by the person who received it. My heart just wanted to help someone else live. The angels showed me that when I pass over to the other side and see my life review, I will see the person who received my kidney and the ripple effect it had on their life. That is enough for me. As I write, it has been four years since I donated my kidney, and I'm still glad that I did it. I hope the recipient is living a full life and gets to enjoy her grandchildren the way I enjoy mine.

About a week and a half after donating, I was back to work and feeling pretty good. Giving myself Reiki really helped the healing process, and I realized it would be a good idea to offer people Reiki before and after surgery. The healing from Reiki was exponential. While I am an advocate for donation, you don't have to donate a kidney to save someone's life. You can simply be there for people, listening to them and helping them. This is lightwork, and it is so beautiful.

7

THE REASON WE ARE HERE

Earlier in the book, I shared that we *chose* to come here to earth and to live in a physical body. We came to learn lessons to be a better soul. In heaven or the other realm, there is no pain or crisis or struggle. We don't even have an actual body to cause us pain and frustration. We are energy beings of light who speak to each other telepathically so there are no words exchanged. We freely communicate in love, joy, and peace. We are not just playing harps on the other side; we have an active life of becoming our highest-vibrating, best soul. Heaven is our real home, and earth is the painful place. Because our soul wants to be in its highest karma or Christ consciousness, we chose to come here and learn lessons that will elevate our wisdom and character. We sat around a heavenly table with the other souls on our soul team and planned the things we would experience here in this life. Souls on our soul team offered to play parts in our experience. Some volunteer to be parents, husbands, or friends to us. They do this because they love us, and we also may play parts for them in their life journey.

There are many different timelines and lives happening at the same time, which is something hard to comprehend. We will understand this when we go back, but it is hard for us in our humanness to understand. We were given a sort of amnesia so we could forget where we came from in order to live the life we chose here. We had to forget our beautiful home to fully live this life. I feel like I am always longing for something, and it may be homesickness. You may have different beliefs, especially if you grew up with a formal religion as I did. I grew up Catholic and became Christian in my life, so it took me a while to reconcile how I felt about this school of thought. I found that it fits perfectly when I imagine the heaven I grew up learning about. When we go back to heaven, we will be back with God/Source at the highest vibration of love. Feel free to disagree with me; I learned this from my angels and guides whom I trust with my whole heart. You always need to trust your soul when it comes to your beliefs.

Energy healers and lightworkers came here with a mission or plan to help balance the human experience. They are like a connection between heaven and earth. They live in a higher vibration and have less amnesia about where they came from. Lightworkers collect light and love from Source, and by helping others, they distribute that light and love to other souls here. Since we came from a place where there is no pain, it is hard to be in a human body. We definitely chose to feel the feelings and downfalls of a human existence. We came here to taste chocolate, to cry, to grieve, and to learn, we came to feel all of it.

Empaths and lightworkers offered to make the human experience easier while they live out their own human experience. This is so compassionate, and only advanced souls would offer this in their time here. As souls, we come in all stages of vibration, so there will be souls that are less evolved and souls that are more evolved. Some who come will not evolve much here, and they may come back to continue their evolution and experience and to learn more lessons. For this reason, even if we feel we are more enlightened or advanced, it does not make us better in any way. There is no ego in heaven, and we don't judge anyone there. If you are very judgmental here, you may be less evolved—only an evolved soul would understand that we are all just on different timelines of learning, and we need to love people where they are on their journey.

It is hard to see people go through difficult experiences, especially the ones we love. Remember that we all choose what we will go through here, and we cannot go through another person's journey for them or save them from the pain they chose in order to elevate. Why would a baby choose to get cancer? It is not fair when people die young, why do we have to lose those we love? I ask these questions all the time. My angels tell me that I will understand when I go back home. So I don't have an answer for you; I too am living this life, and I believe the angels and guides can't explain some things to me in my human form because I would not understand. Here is what I do know.

Love is always the answer and always will be.
We are here to love.
We are here to help.
We are here to learn.
We are here to evolve.
We are here to feel pain.
We are here to heal.

In my fifty-five years here, I have struggled with so many things, but I know that I would never have known what happiness feels like if I hadn't experienced sadness. I would not know what grief feels like if I had not experienced love. I have made huge mistakes, I have hurt people, and I have helped people. My goal for the rest of my time here is to spread love, to teach people that love is the way.

I encourage you to accept and truly embody yourself as a lightworker. Heal yourself and heal others along the way. We don't know how long we have here, so put your emphasis on love. Be present, search for your answers, and don't stop growing. Most of all, *love yourself* unconditionally. Doing so will allow love to overflow out of your spirit. Lightworker, you are so loved!

Sources

Robert Schwartz, *Your Souls Plan*

Anita Moorjani, *Dying to Be Me*
   What If This Is Heaven?
   Sensitive Is the New Strong

Sonia Choquette, *Ask Your Guides*

Kyle Gray, The Angel Guide Oracle, oracle deck

Glennon Doyle and Abby Wambach, *We Can Do Hard Things*
   podcast